Embracing Imperfection:

The Healing Journey of a Suicide Attempt Survivor

This roller coaster ride to recovery from self-injury, suicidal thinking and attempts to finding those moments of emotional balance and inner peace, is dedicated to teens, young adults and their parents

Tracey Pacheco Medeiros, Co-Author

Annemarie Matulis, Co-Author

ISBN: 978-0-9974239-5-2

Acknowledgements

To my mother and father who I wished were here to see this, I love you and miss you. To Annemarie Matulis, the unconditional love you gave me and the path you helped put me on, gave me a second chance in life. I am eternally grateful. To my second family, Annemarie, Eric Newnum, Bill Dexter and especially, George Larkin; I could not have made it through the storm without all of you in my life. Thank you! To Jason, Rachel, Jasper, and Jacob; Jessica, Paul, Blayden, Hailey and Kloie (rest in peace), thank you for always letting me be a part of your family. You gave me strength to keep moving forward. I will love you all, always.

To my Higher Power, thank you for never giving up on me and believing in me when I couldn't. Thank you for letting me find you again. To Douglas Emerson, thank you for never giving up on me. To my dog, Ashes, thank you for loving me unconditionally. When I needed you the most, you were always right there.

To my brothers and sister, each of you helped me to be the person I am today. Thank you.

And I am dedicating this conversation (some call it a book) to all of the teens, young adults and anyone who is a suicide attempt survivor, suffers from constant thoughts of suicide and/or self-injures. Don't give up. You matter.

Table of Contents

Introduction 8

Who Am I? 9

The Flow...11

The Flow 12

Today 14

Where to Begin.. 15

Sanctuary 17

Community Conversations 21

Re-Energize & Re-Connect 24

The Back Story.. 27

The Back Story 28

The Nightmare Begins 30

My Canoe and Fishing...................................... 38

Motorcycle... 40

My Father 41

Punching Bag 43

Being Married & NSSI (Non-Suicidal Self Injury) aka Cutting 44

Those First Steps to Wellness 48

Sharing My Lived Experience 51

Moving On..53

2009 and Rosie 54

That Grand Canyon State of Mind.................... 57

Testing, Testing, Testing 1-2-3......................... 59

Cancer - Annemarie 62

A Time of Conflict, Loss and Hope................... 64

That Pesky "C" Word 70

Random Wrap-Up Thoughts 79

The Home Stretch and Wicked Awesome Wish List 83

The Next Chapter.. 86

One Last Thing 88

References.. 91

Introduction

Who Am I?

I was misdiagnosed, over medicated and dismissed. As an adolescent, I was sexually abused and then ignored when I sought help. Instead of receiving help and support from my parents, I was blamed. By my mid-teens, I was beyond angry, bitter and violent. I tried to fit in, to do the society says dance. My only real relief was sports. I was an excellent athlete throughout high school, but academically, I was just pushed through classes.

And the anger continued to fester wrapped with irrational shame and guilt that it "must have been my fault." The "it" being everything from the abuse as a child, to my grades, to always getting into trouble, to lack of parental support...the pain inside burned like a volcano ready to erupt.

I got married – for all the wrong reasons even though I did love my husband. But there was too much wreckage from the past that I was dragging around emotionally. And on his side, not an ounce of compassion or understanding.

I can't write, not the way other people can, and I struggle with sentence structure and grammar. I hate public speaking. My English is more "street" than academic. My thoughts get jumbled sometimes and I have trouble expressing myself verbally, and I jump all over the place. And yet, I have witnessed and experienced the positive impact that sharing my story has on others when I took the risk to just stand up and share from my heart:

I am a suicide attempt survivor who continues to live with mental health diagnoses, battle breast cancer and all of its chaos and survived (at least, so far) and this is my story.

The Flow

The Flow

There is no real "order of appearance" to this book, because I don't look at it as book. This is my life, my story. If we were sitting across from each other, that's not how I would talk with you. I'd jump all over the place and hope you could keep up with me. I've always been like that. It takes a little getting used to. And some of what you read will overlap with something else, and bits and pieces will be repeated. I tend to repeat myself or, say the same thing a slightly different way.

It was suggested that I stop thinking of this as "writing a book," but just sit down and have a conversation. That conversation has taken about 10 years. Seriously. My mentor encouraged me to do this as a way to clear my head and to be able to put things in order. I've lost count of how many counselors/therapists said, "It might help if you write some of this down."

And can we make this conversation a little easier by allowing me to stop saying "mentor"? Here's how this finally ended up in print: I talked – a lot, and Annemarie wrote it down. That's why it says on the cover, "co-authors." I talk. She writes. She *is* my mentor, my life coach, my second mom, all of that. And this was not a journey I did on my own. I had a lot of help, and Annemarie was a major part of it. So, a lot of what you read will include references to her just like I would if we were hanging out and I was talking to you about all of this. OK? Cool.

So, if you were looking to read some kind of gory, gruesome, sad story, this is the wrong conversation. And it's not rocket science, either. It's a conversation about hope and healing.

What we finally came up with was to create a few sections: *Today, The Back Story*, and *Moving On*, and hopefully fit the pieces of my journey into one of those sections. (laughing out loud) I left that up to Annemarie to figure out.

Today

Where to Begin?

For years, that's the question I asked every time I thought about writing my story. Where the heck do you begin? I've lost count of how many times I said to myself or out loud to Annemarie (never out loud to anyone else), "Where do I begin?"

And since I never came up with an answer, I'd let the negative self-talk just talk me right out of doing anything – for years. My writing sucks. I repeat myself, have no sense of structure, and grammar and punctuation that will make most teachers cringe. So for me to have a finished product takes so much time, like forever.

I had books dropped in front me like Julia Cameron's *The Artist's Way*, and Anne Lamott's *Bird by Bird*. I was told something about "shitty first drafts" were OK and to be expected. I did move *The Artist's Way* around a lot, from one table and bookcase to another. Every once in a blue moon I'd pick it up and browse through it or read a page or two. And my therapist got on the bandwagon, too, with things like,

You might find it helpful to do some journaling.

Have you done any journaling yet, Tracey?

How's the journaling going?

God bless. She did try.

And the writing, journaling, *The Artist's Way* were all tools that those around me were encouraging me to use when my emotions and mental wellness were on yet another roller coaster ride, because if I didn't get focused. I might begin to have suicidal thoughts again (their concern, not mine). I'm sure there's some research project out there that explains why it's so hard for someone with borderline personality disorder or bipolar or PTSD to stay focused. OK, that statement itself should explain it, but when you live with this every day, it's hard to see in that moment. In my heart, I know I can work through whatever the challenge is. I have the coping skills. Hell. I now teach the coping skills…but when the roller coaster storm starts to build in my head, all bets are off. The good news, no – the *great* news is that those storm cloud periods are getting shorter and shorter.

And I think that's one of the driving forces behind why I finally dug in to share my story – it does get better. And by that I mean not only my awareness of the mental health challenges I face every day, but that they control me less and less. I have hope. I don't want to die. I want to live life as fully as I can.

Sanctuary

The word sanctuary never had much meaning to me. It was something other people had. For so much of my life, where I lived was never a sanctuary. Looking back, it's amazing and sad how much of my life I never felt safe anywhere. But that's changed.

In October 2015, as I began aggressive chemotherapy treatments, I moved into the McKinstry House, a 270-year old colonial that serves as the rectory for the Episcopal Church of St. Thomas. (laughing out loud) Yeah, me, living in a rectory. There's a spirit about this house that you have to feel. Words don't do it justice. And there was no better place for me to begin the long process of fighting the breast cancer diagnosis. Complete quiet in the middle of a city. A sanctuary, finally.

The very first morning I woke up there I felt the difference. No yelling. No doors slamming. No tension. Wow! This was a first for me. I have had that feeling of total inner peace before (but not very often). In 2010, Annemarie and I went on a three week "southwest sabbatical," her words not mine. We drove all over the country. I saw the corn fields of Kansas…for an entire day of driving…no wonder Toto didn't want to go home. I always had my eyes out for professional sports stadiums, saw the arch over St. Louis and then, after a more driving we could see the outline of the Rockies in the distance. Another "wow."

By the time we reached Grand Junction, Colorado, and headed into the Badlands, I could feel the transformation I mentioned. A sense of peace and sanctuary. It was like weights had been lifted off my shoulders. No yelling, no fights, no turmoil.

We reached Bryce Canyon late in the afternoon, in time to watch the incredible colors of the canyon as the sun began to set. We spent the entire next day at Bryce, going up, and up and up, and eventually, down. As millions know, words don't work well to describe the canyons and pictures are nice, but not quite the same as being there. After investigating some of the other canyons, we landed on the north rim of the Grand Canyon.

And that's where I had what I refer to as spiritual experience. The weather could not have been more perfect – clear and sunny. I couldn't believe my eyes as I looked out over the canyon. Then, I headed down that can-I-throw-up-now, very narrow trail out to Bright Angel Point. And just stood there. There were a lot of people around me, but I felt like I was the only one. Something physical changed in me, and it wasn't the altitude. I wish I could say that I was able to hold onto that "Grand Canyon" state of mind forever, but I couldn't. I was able to get glimmers of it once in a while.

My life was changing. I was changing. I was healing, a little bit more every day. I'll share more about this in "The Back Story" section but my life was like a roller coaster ride at this time. I was amazed that a local health care agency hired me to work with people who had mental health issues including suicidal ideation and attempts. I kept asking why would a health care agency hire someone with mental health issues to work with people who had mental health concerns? Yeah, you're right. The answer is obvious now. It's called peer to peer and it works.

Peer Specialist was the job title and after a certification process, it was Certified Peer Specialist. I love my job.

In addition to this new job, I had a new therapist and a counselor. After extensive examinations and lots of tests, I also had a completely new diagnosis and major meds changes. After 20 years of hell, I began to feel better. And if I can get your attention about anything, that's one of the most important. Don't just accept the diagnosis and proposed treatment. I grew up in a generation that looked at doctors as gods. That was the culture I raised in. It's wrong and cost me 20 years of my life without the correct diagnosis. It almost killed me.

And this is something I am always talking to teens and young people about – and their parents. I'm not sure why people have the idea that these meds will kick in within 24 hours and everything will be fine. I urge the kids to try to be patient. Depending on the meds, it could take weeks or longer. On the other hand, if you have an immediate and severe negative reaction of some kind, tell the doctor. Always, always be honest with your doctor about how the meds are or are not working. We know our bodies best but it took me years to understand that I had to be my own best advocate.

And it was about this time that I began to really take a long hard look at the coping skills I'd been taught in DBT – **Dialectical behavior therapy** is a specific type of cognitive-behavioral psychotherapy developed in the late 1980s by psychologist Marsha M. Linehan to help better treat borderline personality disorder. Since its development, it has also been used for the treatment of other kinds of mental health disorders. I could go on and on about the benefits of DBT for attempt survivors, those with mental health concerns and…and, their loved ones.

A bunch of us – attempt survivors, loss survivors, and parents of attempt survivors, were hanging out doing some filming for a new documentary and one mom said that after she studied DBT, she realized that she was using the wrong words to try to better communicate with her son. DBT taught her a new way to reach out and have those conversations. I would like to suggest that all parents/family of suicide attempt survivors at least check out DBT.

Community Conversations

A few weeks ago, I was part of a "Community Conversation" locally. Wait, let me back up. I am a member of the Bristol County (MA) Regional Coalition for Suicide Prevention (BCRCSP). One of the things we do is host open sessions in the cities and towns we serve to engage people in conversations about preventing suicide. (I'll share more about how I got into this in *The Back Story* section).

The panel we brought to this event was myself, as an attempt survivor, and Steve Palm, who is a loss survivor. Our third speaker, Kathy Nemkovich, a loss survivor, was not able to join us. We're kind of a team and we speak about how working together has helped all of us move forward along the healing path…and I'll talk more about that in the *Moving On* section. I did say there was overlap. The other two members on the panel were Jacquie O'Brien, the chair for the Greater Attleboro Suicide Prevention Coalition, and Annemarie, who is the director of the BCRCSP.

There were about 38 people there. Parents, some teens, the local cable access station was filming it and the police and fire chiefs for the town were there, which is amazing. Not only did they come, they did the welcoming remarks, stayed for the entire event, and even stayed after the event to talk with people.

My point here is what happens when we do these events. As Steve and I share our personal journeys, we cross over to share how for me, I was impacted the first time I heard a loss survivor share her story, and Steve shared how he was impacted the first time he heard me share mine. It's powerful to have attempt survivors and loss survivors together.

Let me back up a bit. In 2009, we held our first AFSP (American Foundation for Suicide Prevention) International Survivors Day at our teen center. Rosie Walisever shared her story of losing her son Adam to suicide while he was in college. I could not stop crying and I could barely breathe. It was the first time I had sat down up close and personal with a loss survivor and really listened. I was stunned. The first thought was "I almost did that to my family!" Rosie and I have become friends. I am so grateful that she was there that day and I was able to hear her words and feel her pain. It was life-changing. I experienced some dark days after that and when suicidal thoughts crossed my mind (no plan, just thoughts), so did Rosie's voice.

Last spring (2016), I came home from another chemo treatment and it happened to be the night that the Kitchen Table Grief Support Conversation for suicide loss survivors was meeting in the house. I stopped by to say hello and they asked me to sit down for a bit. Somehow, I was asked about what was going on in mind before my last attempt and if I would share that with them. So, I did.

I shared about the depth of my despair and hopelessness, and the unbearable inner pain. But I also shared that I was not thinking in terms of how suicide would impact my family. It never crossed my mind. It's tunnel vision at that point. I needed the pain to stop and I saw no other option. I excused myself so they could get on with their session but I worried that I may have offended someone or hurt them with my honesty. I later discovered that just the opposite happened. Steve and other broke down in tears, but they were tears of relief. Steve said that he felt as if concrete block had been lifted off his shoulders. Annemarie said that you could see a physical change in him right then and there, a positive one.

Kathy and I had already done a couple of community conversations together the year before. This was the second time Steve and I had done it. The response from the audience confirmed for us that we're doing the right thing. Hearing the lived experience from both perspectives and then hearing how we benefit from doing this helps the people in the audience to begin their own conversation.

So, the three of us, Steve, Kathy and myself are scheduled to present this interaction at our state conference in a few weeks. We'll let you know how it went.

The Re-Energize & Re-Connect Wellness Check Workshops

Yeah, that's a mouthful, for sure. But after just talking about why I feel it's so important for attempt survivors and loss survivors to work together and encourage people to sit down and talk about preventing suicide, we need to step back and talk about the R&RWP.

I am not a grant writer and wouldn't know where to begin. And I certainly am not someone to create a curriculum, but Annemarie does both.

While she was producing and filming the documentary *A Voice at the Table*, she really paid attention to what the four of us who were in the film said about not having resources available to us after our suicide attempts. The four I'm referring to are Dese'Rae L. Stage, Cara Anna, Craig Miller and myself. So Annemarie began to outline a program for suicide attempt survivors who were further along the healing path. Shortly after she started that, the Department of Public Health's Suicide Prevention Program (that's who she works for) released a grant opportunity to develop "new and innovative support programs" for suicide attempt survivors and loss survivors.

The BCRCSP, through Annemarie, partnered with the agency I work for, Community Counseling of Bristol County, and together they submitted a grant that included two versions of the R&RWP: one for attempt survivors and one for loss survivors. That was February 2014.

We were awarded the grant, spent the first year developing the curriculum and protocols, and held our first series of workshops in August 2015. It was exciting to know that three other regional coalitions also received awards to do attempt survivor programs. Knowing that we have a huge number of attempt survivors all around us, I was surprised that each of the locations had only a few actually step up to do the programs. The other three programs were initially for those who had a recent attempts, but either way, I really hoped we'd have a large number come forward. That still hasn't happened yet, but we have all continued to host our respective programs.

And I'm glad we did continue with the R&RWP. I enjoy being a co-facilitator, and have learned a lot about what the behind the scenes stuff of running a grant is like – the reports and the tracking, although Annemarie does all that, but I had never been involved with that end of programs before. We made constant revisions as we went along and then I introduced coloring because I find it helps me focus.

So what is a spiritual wellness check workshop for suicide attempt survivors? It's a little bit of 12 Step modality, a dash of DBT (Dialectical Behavior Therapy), some mindfulness, and some personal inventory. And we share a lot about how we handle a crisis or how we respond to good things happening. We call it the "What did you do when…" this or that happened. It's about healthy coping skills.

After a year, some loss survivors asked if they could begin their own series. So, we did, but within a few months, we brought together a focus group from both groups – attempt and loss survivors, and the result was that we all agreed, we should simply all come to the same table. So, we do. Once a month for about a five month stretch. Then we take a break and come back again for another 5-6 month series. And that's how we came to ask Steve if he would like to join our community conversation panels. We were all sitting around coloring and talking about anger that night, I think, and Steve expressed an interest in being more public to help other families.

So, our next steps with the R&RWP is to have a consistent youth group in place and to host a Train the Facilitator so other folks can bring this to their communities. Above all, this is a resilience based, protective factor – the ultimate goal is to prevent suicide.

The Back Story

The Back Story

I love back stories. Wherever Annemarie and I go, even if it's just shopping, when we pass a car or some people on the street, I create a back story. We did this all the way to Denver and back when we presented a workshop at the Colorado Suicide Prevention Summit in 2015. And I had a field day when we drove into Boston for almost a year during my chemotherapy. I wasn't able to drive, so our friend George did, and we'd check out all the people we went by during the morning commute (most of whom were on their cell phones either talking or texting) and then, when we hit the city, we had all the people running to catch trolleys, trains and buses or waiting at bus stops. Lots of "back stories." It was awesome.

You know, what I mean right? I'll bet you all do it, too. You drive by someone who looks so sad, all slumped over at the wheel and stuff. *So, why is he sad? Maybe he hates his job? Or he just wanted to stay cuddled up in bed? Or he didn't get that promotion?* Right? And those crews at the bus stop. No joke. Ten to twelve people at the same bus stop every week and they never talked with each other. Not once did we ever catch them actually talking to one another. Just chilling as if they're all alone, headsets on or head bent down to their phones, or just staring into space, bus stop after bus stop. Kind of sad, actually. I always wondered, who are they, what's their back story? *Are they happy? What kinds of jobs do they have?*

And because of who I am and what my life is about, I can't help but wonder,

"How many have attempted suicide, or struggled with suicidal thoughts, or self-injury? Have they told anyone? Have they tried to get help? Are they healing and recovering now?"

I mean, you can't exactly just jump out the car and ask those questions. But maybe we should? We need to do more to open the door to allow people to speak up and feel that it's OK, that they are OK to talk about what's going on. People have the slightest chest pain and we jump all over them to get to a doctor assuming it's a heart attack. For a long time, public health has pushed the thought that everyone should know how to apply CPR.

Yet we stand by silent when someone is thinking about suicide. That's just wrong.
When are we going to put that same challenge out there about mental health issues and suicide?

But I digress (laughing out loud). I do that a lot.
So the chapters that follow give you some insight to my back story.

The Nightmare Begins

I'd love to say that my childhood was normal. When I look back, it sucked. I was seven or eight the first time I was molested and too scared to tell anyone. I went to church. I went to Sunday school. My mother wanted me to be like my sister and take tap dance lessons and become a child model. I tried that and hated it. Then I found little league baseball – not, softball, *baseball*. The real deal. And I was able to escape my fears on the field. But that only helped for a little while. At twelve, I finally went to my mother to tell her what was happening to me. Her reaction?

"What did you do to cause that?" She blamed *me*!

(*Now, I need to pause here. That was a long time ago and I have learned to accept that my mom did the best she could with what she had to work with. Her generation just didn't know how to deal with that kind of stuff. I love her and I know **today** that she always loved me.*)

My world crashed. Where was God? Why was it my fault? I didn't do anything wrong. And the rejection and fear and pain just grew. I existed in my own little hell and that young became convinced that I was a bad person, no good, and whatever happened to me was my fault. And every once in a while, on a really bad day, those thoughts can still terrorize me – for moment.

In high school, I threw myself into sports. I also threw myself into a few other things like drugs and alcohol, the wrong crowd, really bad behavior in class, and worst of all, considering the work I do now as an adult – I became a bully. Other kids were afraid of me.

There was no mental health support like most schools have today. I was a disaster waiting to happen but no one ever asked why I was so angry. My grades were really bad but teachers literally passed me on to the next level so they didn't have to deal with my anger and outbursts. After all, I was a star athlete, and we can't have her failing, can we? Out of nowhere, I began to have seizures. The tests didn't seem to explain why, so the doctors said I had epilepsy. All that did was make me feel even more like a loser, like a freak. I walked away from my church. As far as I was concerned, God had abandoned me or maybe I just wasn't good enough for Him to love me. And the internal pain just grew and grew, but I told no one. That silence almost killed me. Somewhere between my junior and senior years, I attempted suicide. I woke up in the morning and never told anyone.

I wasn't without dreams. I wanted to be a cop, like my oldest brother, or join the military and be part of the military police. I told my mother and she immediately shot me down insisting the military wouldn't take me because of my seizures. She was right and I got angrier. I approached the local police chief about joining the force but the answer was the same – not with seizures.

I threw myself into one job after another, work, work, and work - to make sure I could pay my bills. That would prove I was perfect. But I also partied pretty hard for a few years. Emotionally, I was a mess and worried that maybe I should try to get some help. At nineteen, I went to my first therapist. I didn't like her and thought she was snob who had no clue what I was trying to tell her and I was right.

I got hurt on the job one day. My knee got all twisted up and I had to use crutches. When I told her what happened, she immediately accused me of intentionally trying to hurt myself and picked up the phone to section me into a hospital. I went ballistic when she said she was sending me to a psychiatric lock up so I couldn't hurt myself. I couldn't believe this was happening. I got hurt on the job!

I couldn't get out of there fast enough but when I did, there were three cop cars and six officers, hands on guns, standing ready to take me down. I was stunned. When they saw me hobble out on crutches, they stood there and stared. Yeah, this was their big "threat." A five-foot nothing, nineteen year old on crutches. A couple of them helped me get into a cruiser and took me to the local hospital. It took hours before that hospital got an ambulance to take me to the state hospital. They got lost on the way, so I told them how to get there. Yup, I was a real threat to myself and to them. That was my second experience seeking help for the pain I was in. The first was when I was molested. Never again.

For the next 10 years, I vowed I would never, ever tell anyone how I was really feeling or thinking. I had no idea what was wrong with me but hell would freeze over before I would ask anyone for help. The struggle to keep a lid on my rage was a daily battle. I broke a lot of things, including my hands more times than I can count from punching things so I didn't punch people.

I applied for a position as a corrections officer. They didn't care about my seizures. For the first time in my life, except for sports, I felt like "someone." I could have a career. I was walking on air. Three years into the job, I got seriously hurt. My co-worker and I were making security rounds and we found a breach – one of the gates wasn't locked properly. While I tried to force it shut, something happened and it rolled over on my leg, crushing me knee. After multiple surgeries and a long rehab effort, the doctor said I could never run or jump from leg to leg again. That meant that I had to retire. I honestly felt like me life was over.

Years later, I recognized the depth of my emotional pain and how I had misdirected it as a C.O. I brought that high school bully to work. I was particularly intolerant of and abusive toward women who had been convicted of child abuse. No one needs a degree in psychology to figure this one out. I was reacting to my own childhood abuse. The women I got along with and could even laugh with were those in prison for prostitution. They were broken, abused and imperfect, just like me.

After a battle with the state over my injury, I went to community college and achieved an Associate's Degree in Culinary Arts. It turns out I'm a great cook, baker and ice sculptor. Who knew? Sadly, the voices in my head still told me I was stupid and worthless. I didn't have skills to turn that around, yet. So, the self-medication increased drastically. If only I could find some way to not feel anything. That volcano I mentioned earlier began to rumble.

I was about to step into my 30's, had a good job as a baker and was in love. And then the walls began to crumble. My dad got really sick. One of my brother's bullied me into believing it would make my dad happy to see me married. Don't get me wrong. I loved this man and I really loved his kids. I just wasn't sure I was ready for marriage. My dad was a proud man and refused to use his oxygen to walk me down the aisle. They had to start the "Wedding March" three times before I was able to hold him tight enough so he wouldn't fall down. We didn't dance to *Butterfly Kisses,* I gently rocked him back and forth. A short time later, he passed. And the volcano inside me erupted.

That first year or so of marriage I was happy. I was upbeat, loved my husband, loved having the step kids around, work was going well. But after my father died, I fell apart. It was like I was rolling down a hill and couldn't stop. The flashbacks came back, day and night. When my husband touched me or reached out to hug or kiss me, I was revolted. He looks nothing like my molester, but he had a beard and dark hair too, and to me, I saw one and the same.

I tried to work through the PTSD with a punching bag. I would spend hours kickboxing and hammering that damn bag with my molester's face in my head, and actually pinned to the wall. But that wasn't enough. The internal pain increased. And that's when I began to cut, and cut…

When people asked me about the scars, I got more tattoos to cover them. But it wasn't enough.

The suicide attempts came fast and furious. One hospital lock up after another. One diagnosis after another. One more bottle of pills after another, all of them wrong (I would learn later).

I tried so hard to be well, to be "good." I put down the drugs and booze, I went back to work, I tried my best to play "house." I went back to counseling. But the pain inside deepened. It was more than I could deal with. I gave up. I went to my father's grave and curled up on the ground and waited to die. The police found me unconscious. I woke up in the hospital.

Choosing life did not come easy. Over the next two years I would hire and fire several counselors. I couldn't hold down a job. The rage was still there. I was still smashing things.

And then came the divorce. On one hand I was devastated; on the other I felt a sense of relief.

I went for almost a year with no meds, no counselor ready to lock me up and, frankly, I didn't do too badly. Inevitably, I began to feel the fear and anxiety again, I was hearing voices again, the PTSD kicked in again. More importantly, I was having suicidal thoughts again but there was a difference this time – I no longer wanted to die.

I saw a new psychiatrist who blew my mind when she said the good news was that I was not clinically depressed; however, I was bipolar, had borderline personality disorder and PTSD. She slowly started me on a careful regimen of totally different meds. And what a difference that made after almost 20 years of hell. My entire life changed.

With Annemarie's support I got involved with youth and the community at large through participation in coalitions for violence prevention and suicide prevention. We also have a program on cable access. A local health care agency offered me a job. They wanted me, with mental health concerns, to work with other people with mental health concerns. I had to take the certification test a couple of times but I am a state certified peer specialist working with people with co-occurring disorders.

On my job, I deal with some aspect of mental health and suicide issues every day. Who better than an attempt survivor, peer to peer can do that? Who better can understand the stigma feared if we speak out. I had a recent run in with that…I have breast cancer and had to have a double mastectomy, and when I shared that last August, people tripped over themselves to offer help – they all wanted to help me – to cook, to clean, to drive me places, whatever I needed. Coming home from chemo, I had a hissy-fit, totally blew up. In tears, I screamed, "Where the hell were all of you when I wanted to die?" I finally met STIGMA face to face. And I began to feel a determination I hadn't felt since playing ball. I now know my life matters and I need to step out of the dark and shatter the silence. And I have. I've done some PSA's, participated in film, and served as the advisor for new, way outside the box resilience workshops for attempt survivors, programs I wish I had available not only when I was struggling but also as I was healing.

But as I said earlier, I can't write, not the way other people can, and I struggle with sentence structure and grammar. I hate public speaking. My English is more "street" than academic. My thoughts get jumbled sometimes and I have trouble expressing myself verbally. And yet, I have witnessed and experienced the positive impact that sharing my story has on others when I continue to take the risk to stand up and share from my heart:

My Canoe and Fishing

I started fishing at an earlier age with my brother Ricky. In fact, he was the one who taught me how to fish. At first, he would help me with the hooks and bait and even take the fish off for me. After a while he would always take me fishing with him around the local area. He only taught me how to bobber fish and I didn't learn about trolling and bottom fishing until I was in my late twenties and fishing with my ex-husband.

I can't explain it well, but I really loved fishing. The chaos in my head would quiet down because I had to be patient, and wait to attract the fish. And practicing that helped me find a little bit of relief with the inside stuff. I felt safe surrounded by the water, sometimes looking like glass if there was no wind, and the birds coming and going. I would stay out there for hours.

One summer I wanted to buy a canoe because I couldn't afford a boat and at the time, my vehicle was suitable for the canoe. I took it out every weekend I could, including when I was on vacation. It was the most peaceful thing that I had ever did. At first, I just would paddle around but then I decided to get back to fishing in the canoe.

So, my fishing meant that I was a "catch and release" person. It was great to have the time to do the both things that I like to do. But as time went by, the fishing license got to be so expensive that I just didn't want to bother for the weekends anymore. And then I lost interest in fresh water fishing, but I still enjoyed canoeing on the lake. That continued to help me calm down and feel a little bit of inner peace. But then, my friend who lived on the lake moved and I nowhere to keep my canoe. I ended up selling it. I really miss both of those activities. I guess you could say they were part of my wellness plan and coping skills.

Motorcycle

Since I was a little kid, I wanted to ride a motorcycle. In my teenage years, I rode a scooter until it died. Then I didn't bother getting another one because, as I got older, I wanted something bigger and better. And when they changed the driving laws about scooters, that you have to get a motorcycle license to drive one, I was like, no way am I doing that. If I have to get my license, then I'm going to get a motorcycle.

But by that time, I'd been injured on the job and my knees were seriously damaged (and eventually, both had to be replaced). I knew they needed to be strong to hold up and move a heavy bike around, so I thought that was never going to be an option.

I kept on seeing my brothers get their licenses, buy themselves motorcycles, and I would get really angry, in part because they would always tease me and actually put me down, making it clear that in their opinion, I would never be able to have my own bike. And that was kind of the relationship we had. To them I was still that little kid. I was so resentful about all of this that even when I saw a woman riding a motorcycle, I was angry and jealous. Not a healthy state of mind, but during those years, there really wasn't much about my mind that was healthy. Looking back at my risky behavior and deep-rooted anger, it's probably a good idea I wasn't on a motorcycle.

There is more to this story and I'll share that in the *Moving On* section.

My Father

I loved my husband but we got married because I gave in to the pressure my brother put on me to make my father happy. My father was very ill and getting worse all the time. We expected him to die any day, probably during our honeymoon.

The day I got married, they had to start the Wedding March three times because my father couldn't walk, he couldn't move. He refused to use his oxygen tank to walk me down the aisle. Everyone was looking at him, staring at him...I grabbed his arm as tightly as I could and held him up as we crawled down the aisle. Everyone just stared. Not how I pictured that walk down the aisle we dream about. When they played "Butterfly Kisses," he couldn't dance. He could barely stand up, so I gently rocked him back and forth, and cried.

I can't say that I knew my father well. He worked and worked and worked to pay all the bills for six kids. I think that's why my oldest brother and his wife kind of "adopted" me. They took me everywhere with them, Ricky taught me to fish, not my dad, all that kind of stuff. And I was really grateful for all the attention that he and his wife, Janet, showered on me. I knew they cared.

My father got very, very ill. I fell apart when he died. My world crashed. I was in shock and really don't remember much about the wake or funeral or the next few weeks. Then, all the shit that I'd stuffed down so deep for 15 or16 years began to surface.

Punching Bag

Somewhere after my father died, I was back in therapy and my therapist had suggested that I hit a pillow when the old memories of abuse would come up, triggering so much anger. I thought, "Why?" What's the point in doing that? I just felt that was really stupid.

So I got a punching bag. And I would tape a picture on my abuser to it and just wail away, slamming that bag over and over again until my hands hurt. I guess this might be the right time to mention that being suicidal was not the only concern my therapist had. I was deemed to be homicidal. Now that's a scary thing to know when you are fully aware of how much rage you're trying to keep a lid on.

My husband had no idea how angry I was and he had no clear idea why my therapist recommended that I spend hours whacking a punching bag. And that made me angry, too. I loved him and had this silly hope that he would protect me, and hold me and tell me it will all be OK. But he just couldn't seem to find it in himself to give the comfort I so needed and wanted.

So, I'd hit the damn bag harder. At some point, I just stopped. It wasn't helping any more.

Being Married & NSSI

(Non-Suicidal Self Injury)

Aka Cutting

I had boyfriends throughout high school but I didn't get married until I was 30. It only lasted three years. I was OK married. I was upbeat most of the time, we bought a house and I really loved my step-kids. They were actually in the wedding. And I can honestly say I loved my husband but I also know now that I got married for all the wrong reasons – to please other people, to make other people happy. I think I shared this already but I gave in to the pressure from one of my brothers. My father was terminally ill and the manipulation was that it would make him so happy to see his youngest daughter married before he died. When I think about it, I never recall my father ever saying that to me.

And I can step back and say that I know I was not perfect or always easy to be around with my good, bad and ugly mental health days. But I truly did the best I could. Helping to take care of Jason and Jessica, my step-children was really a joy. I am so grateful to have had that opportunity and to still have them in my life today.

The entire year after my father's death is a blur. I was married, helped take care of my step kids, worked full time, self-medicated a lot, and somewhere in that year I began to cut. And I'm not even sure on why I chose that either.

It's really hard to explain or describe what it feels like inside. I was a mess. I was in so much pain internally, emotionally and I just didn't know what to do with it. I was hearing voices and then the nightmares started – flashbacks about the abuse. I'd wake up with terrified that it was happening all over again, and I'd be soaked from the sweats.

I was always trapped in this horrible sense of fear and impending doom, and it was being triggered by the intimacy in my marriage. I'm sure it sounds weird but my husband looked a little like my abuser had when he was younger – the beard, his hair. It started to freak me out.

Somewhere at the end of that first year after my father died, I ended up being hospitalized for the cutting. The one good thing that came from this was a man I met who would become my counselor. I was certainly a challenge.

I thought it was safe now, that it would be OK to talk to my husband about what was bothering me. He was my husband. We were married. The whole "in sickness and in health" deal. But he got angry and pushed back at me. He thought I was saying there was something wrong with him sexually. But there wasn't. I was being triggered.

After a while, things got worse and he got angrier. He went off on me. He accused me of sleeping with other men and then, he accused me of sleeping with women. He got really mean and said I was too fat, that I must be gay if I didn't want to have sex with him. Then he accused me of having sex with my therapist.

Over the next two years, I struggled. There were times I was OK for a while. Having the kids around helped me focus. I loved taking care of them. But then the nightmares would start up again. My husband and I got further and further apart. I met people who were trying to help me to stop self-medicating and he resented anyone who was trying to help me get well.

I don't know. Maybe the relationship was doomed from the start. We had lived together for almost 8 years before we got married. And we had some bumps in there but things got worse pretty quickly. I was experiencing constant flash backs about the sexual abuse. I have no idea what my father's death had to do with it, maybe the grief opened me up?

There was more cutting, more suicide attempts, more hospitalizations and no one close to me had a clue as to why. Even when I tried to tell them, they just pushed it aside like I was exaggerating or making it all up. I tried. I really tried to get well.

I finally shared some of this with Annemarie and she very quietly said, "Tracey, that's abuse." I didn't want to hear it, not again. I was back in the hospital. I was so alone and isolated. I was so damn tired of the pain. I was tired of cutting. It no longer gave me any relief. I was tired of crying myself to sleep believing it was all my fault, that I was just too stupid to fix things. I was just so tired. I was done

I went to my father's grave and curled up to die.

By God's grace, the police found me in time, just in time. And that was almost 18 years ago. I guess I had a little hope. I called my husband and said goodbye and I called Annemarie to thank her for trying to help me. They both called the police. That was my last suicide attempt.

When I finally came home, my husband informed me that he wanted a divorce. Only later did I find out he had already been seeing someone else. I was stunned, devastated. Once again, it must have been my fault. Those were some very dark days, and although I was depressed, and had suicidal thoughts, I did not take any action.

Those First Steps to Wellness

The next few months are a blur. Something inside was different. Don't misunderstand, I wasn't exactly thrilled to be alive but I wasn't sure I really wanted to die. One piece of me wanted to get well, really, really well. I wasn't sure I could.

And then came the divorce.

I was angry, shocked, I guess. We had said vows. Those people who tried to help me once before were right there again and walked me through the next year. It wasn't easy and I was hell to be around most of the time. Years of anger just kept spilling over everywhere. I pissed off a lot of people. I just stumbled along, day after day.

Annemarie and some other friends circled around me and literally walked me through every day for several months. She even found volunteer work for me to do at one of her jobs (laughing out loud). I'm sure her real goal was to keep me within her sight. But it worked. I slowly began to put one foot in front of the other.

And I couldn't hold down a job. I'm a great worker, really, but the anger got in the way. I just couldn't handle the whole "authority" thing. I know now that it all went back to the abuse and then the divorce, but at the time, I was just in a rage and hit back the minute anyone told me what to do or criticized something I did.

It took another year of emotional and mental deterioration to give in and give up – a little, anyway (not completely). The flashbacks and voices came back. With help from my new, small group of "family," and as much as I hated to do it, I filed for SSDI to allow myself time to get well and find the right path to follow, because I didn't have a clue about who I was any more, and that's a scary place to be. I went to the Massachusetts Rehabilitation Commission and was given a grant to upgrade my computer skills.

But things did not go all that well for the next few years. What I know now and keep repeating so others can really examine what they are experiencing – I was misdiagnosed and over medicated with the wrong meds! Again, I now know that a huge part of that was being on the wrong meds. They made me more aggressive. They brought on suicidal thinking again.

I thank God that my small circle of friends, my second family, never gave up on me. I finally hit a space where things calmed down for a bit. After a lot of thought and worrying, I applied to UMass Dartmouth as a full time psychology student. And I was accepted! I spent week constantly blurting out, "*I'm going back to school!*" to anyone who would listen. I was really excited. I walked into my first class and realized that I was the oldest one in the class.

It was a battle to get through my courses. I was never a good student in high school and I'm still amazed that I pulled off my Associates Degree in

Culinary Arts. But full time psychology was like jumping in the ocean not knowing how to swim. I plodded along, barely keeping a GPA high enough to remain in class. My mental health battles just continued to show up and disrupt what I was trying to do. And then I managed an A in Statistics and thought, OK, maybe I can do this. But I couldn't. I had another knee replacement that took me away from an entire semester and then my mom was diagnosed with lung cancer. I took an extended medical leave from school.

The negative self-talk plagued me: *You're a loser. You're stupid. You'll never go back.*

Sharing My Lived Experience

About two years after the divorce, I began to do some community based service work. Or, the real story is, Annemarie has this really bad habit of taking long walks. When she does, her brain goes into gear and she always comes back with a "new idea." In the summer of 2003, after one of those walks and some stuff in the papers, she called me and our partner in crime, George, and said, no joke: *"So, what are the two of you doing for the rest of your lives?"*

Neither of us was quick enough to think of an answer and so began our journey with Southeastern Massachusetts Voices Against Violence (SEMA-VAV), a grass-roots, all volunteer coalition. For the next 4 years, we did a lot of public awareness, held events and some trainings focused on domestic violence. As you can imagine, it helped me to look within at my entire life, do some emotional house cleaning and let go of some, but not all of the anger and resentment. I loved helping people in this situation. I loved being able to make them laugh. It helped me to begin to heal.

A couple of years after we launched the coalition, we were holding a vigil on the Green to honor National Crime Victims Rights' Week. A reporter had spoken with some others and then came over to me and asked why I was there, why was this important to me. I blurted out that I had been molested as a child by a family member and hoped that standing up in public would give other victims the courage to do the same. Well, that hit the front page of the local paper the next day. Needless to say, all hell broke loose in my family, but I didn't care. It was important for me to stop hiding, to break the silence. Another baby step forward in healing.

About 4 years later, we had a double header. First, Annemarie shared with George and I that we were going to open a teen center for youth on the fringe and at risk (of course we were!), and a few months later, she told me we were going to the Massachusetts Conference for Suicide Prevention. It was something about applying for a grant but they didn't get it and she wanted to go find out why and what we could do to help anyway.

I honestly can't recall much about that conference except I came away feeling as strongly as she did. We had to do something. And these several years of overseeing a teen center, multiple events for domestic violence and teen dating violence helped me to continue to heal.

I have a clear connection with the kids. I'm a gamer, they know my tats cover self-injury scars, and I'm approachable. And, eventually, we began to talk about suicidal thoughts. In 9 years, we've done a number of interventions and not once did one of our kids have to get locked up in a psych unit at that time. Some have been hospitalized since but all received strong support from us and always return to touch base and let us know how they are doing. They helped me far more than anything I did for them.

And I'll leave that there for now.

Moving On

2009 and Rosie

I'm guessing you figured out by now that I really meant it when I said this was a conversation and not a typical "book." And that I jump around a lot.

In the first year of our community based suicide prevention task force, we held some meetings to do stuff that I don't always "get," but I sit there and nod my head and take notes sometimes. (laughing out loud). I am not a student of strategic plans, logic models and action plans. What I want to know is how can I help someone not die by suicide? How can I help someone make the decision to live? That stuff I'm good at. And I'm really good at organizing.

I know I've shared some of this but I think it might help to hear the whole story. So when we agreed to hold an AFSP (American Foundation for Suicide Prevention) International Survivors Day at our new teen center, I was on it. We advertised, got the food and had a full house that day. We had two speakers. The second one was Rosie Walisever, a loss survivor. Rosie and her husband came to our very first Greater Taunton Suicide Prevention Task Force meeting in July of that year (2009) and had continued to hang out with us to be of whatever help she could.

We all sat around in chairs, on the gym floor, and then Rosie stood up to face us and it got very, very quiet. For the next 20 minute or so, she shared her story of losing her son, Adam, to suicide when he was in college, not much older than most of the kids sitting around me. As I listened, I could feel the tears begin. I was stunned. I was a suicide attempt survivor and years into my healing and recovery, I was hearing the pain and agony of a mother who lost her son to suicide. I could barely breathe.

When she finished, we all stood up an applauded. One of our teens walked over, he towered over Rosie, and he said, "*My name is Adam. Thank you for sharing your story with us*," and gave her a huge hug.

Hearing her story was life-changing for me. I often share that she actually may have saved my life because in my darkest moments since then, I hear her voice. The second part of this is that except for Annemarie, I had not told anyone, and definitely had not said publicly that I was a suicide attempt survivor. It was almost like if I didn't say it, it wasn't real. It was now and has been ever since.

That was a major milestone. I would love to say that everything from that day forward was just awesome. Yeah, no. But some good things did begin to happen. The following month a bunch of us completed a QPR (Question, Persuade, Refer) gatekeeper train the trainer. That was my first exposure to formal prevention training and I have to admit that some of the process was a little uncomfortable as an attempt survivor. I started a new job as a peer specialist with a local health care provider. I loved it then and I still love it today. My life was far from perfect but I was pretty busy between working full time and my volunteer work. I was moving on from the wreckage of my past.

And maybe that's one thing that I can strongly encourage anyone who has self-injured, struggles with suicidal thinking or has attempted suicide to consider. Give some thought to volunteering with a local, regional or state suicide prevention coalition. Get involved. Not only can you make a difference in someone's life, you really will feel better yourself. And I would make the same suggestion to the families of attempt survivors and the others. It really helps to break down the isolation.

That Grand Canyon State of Mind

As I think I noted somewhere already, Annemarie suggested that we take a three week "Southwest Sabbatical" to some places she had been to but I never had. I was just glad to get away for a while. But I have to admit, this trip was another life-changing milestone for me. And anyone who has traveled through the Rockies, into Utah and Arizona, and all the canyons there and then to the Grand Canyon itself, knows that pictures and words just aren't good enough to describe the experience. The magnitude and beauty left me speechless and left me feeling grateful that I was alive to have the experience. That is such an important thought for a suicide attempt survivor.

There is no doubt in my mind that there is something powerful and spiritual in that part of our country. The trip also brought us to San Antonio and we visited the Alamo. Looking at everything there, it was so obvious that those men knew they were going to die and continued to fight anyway. I've seen the movies more times than I can count, but it was different to actually stand there, almost as if their spirits were with us. Again, gratitude that I was alive to have that experience.

But something else happened on that trip. Annemarie began to get sick. She had somehow pulled muscles or something. We had no idea how serious it was and she also began to have problems with the altitude. We both brushed it off but it would come back to haunt her and have a profound impact on me.

ne positive side, that three week trip showed me that I really could interact with people over a period of time and not have one argument. That may not mean much to many people, but it impressed the hell out of me. Only a few years earlier, I was unemployable because I was so argumentative and defensive about everything due to misdiagnosis and overmedication. The frustration for me sometimes is that I did not really begin to experience a good quality of life until I was in my 40's because of all that medical mess.

Testing, Testing, Testing 1-2-3

So, I'm not going to list every medication that I was given from the age of 15 to today, but

let's be clear, some of them did some damage. And every once in a while that really ticks me off when I am reminded, like when I'm trying to learn new things or prepare for a test.

Just as refresher, my current diagnosis is, ta dah! Borderline Personality Disorder (for which there is no medication), PTSD, Bipolar Disorder and Depression. I also take medication for seizures. They started in my teens and tests could not clarify why, so I was told I had Epilepsy. No one ever proved that but I still take the meds because everyone, including me, worries about seizures. I haven't had one in about 20 years.

What this all means, and I cannot even imagine how many other folks are in the same boat, is that all this medication combined with my diagnoses, leave my short term memory skills a mess and my ability to learn and process new information can be a challenge, but I can do it. My brain shuts down when there is too much information thrown at me. And with my mental health issues, that can leave me stuck in a whole lot of negative self-talk. And that, in itself, is depressing.

Let me give you an example of how my brain can short-circuit. I study, for hours, make flash cards, study some more, can rattle off answers. Then sit down to take a written test and not be able to recall the material and not do well on the exam. Yet I can sit and talk with you about the exact same material and rattle off the correct answers. The destructive, negative self-talk will shout out to me that I am stupid. I know I'm not but it has taken years for me to learn to turn that around quickly. And, in part, I have to give credit to Dr. Marsha Linehan and DBT.

It took me three exams over 2 years to finally achieve my Certified Peer Specialist status. With no arrogance intended, I can teach that course but I struggled with the testing process. I experience anxiety and self-doubt and I almost gave up. And again, I really believe it's important to talk about this stuff so others who are attempt survivors and/or have this kind of diagnosis are aware that giving up is not an option. I am living proof of why not to give up.

In between my second and third CPS exams, Annemarie and I went up to Canada for a one week training to become ASIST trainers (Applied Suicide Intervention Skills Training). I was again battling negative self-talk (*What were you thinking? You can't do this*!). But I was able to use the training videos to help me get through the process. I am a visual learner. The testing is all hands on (oral). I did it! And I use that achievement when negative self-talk creeps into my brain. My push back is "*I passed the ASIST T4T. Shut Up negativity!*"

Now this may all sound good, all nice and neat in this conversation, but it can actually be a bit messy as it happens. I do have some minor hissy fits about this stuff now and again, but the good news is that they are very short lived. A few years ago, they could last for days and I'd probably have burned any bridges to fixing the problem along the way. And that's because I am on the correct medication and the proper dosage, I am getting older (laughing out loud) and more "mature," and because if I expect the people I work with to use their coping skills, I need to make sure I use my own.

And just so you know, in November of 2016, I returned to college to complete my degree in psychology with a focus on addictions. I'm doing this one online course, one semester at a time. And I'm getting A's! Some things take time but please don't give up. You do matter.

Cancer – Annemarie

I'm not going to talk a lot about this but it had a profound impact on me. It is her story to tell in detail.

After we got back from the Grand Canyon tour, Annemarie got worse and worse. Doctors told her she had done some serious damage to her leg muscles and ligaments. I have two artificial knees, so I know a little bit about that kind of pain. But something else was going on. The muscle spasms got worse and worse, not better. She began to lose weight, a lot of weight. And I began to have some serious anxiety.

There were times I really needed to talk to her about "stuff" but I didn't want to burden her or bother her, so I stayed quiet, and I stayed away. A lot of people did the same thing. We were all in shock watching her become sick. This was Annemarie, our Rock of Gibraltar, the one we all went to in need.

I felt confused, and helpless, and angry, and frightened. What if she dies? She had lost more than 100 pounds and had to use a wheel chair. We got her to the emergency room and they said she would have died if she had not come in. They pumped six units of blood into her. The tests showed cancer. When I went to pick her up 3 days later, I was shocked again, and I didn't know whether to laugh or cry. She was running up and down the hall, up and down stairs, (no wheelchair) muttering something about how amazing blood transfusions can be. She had her surgery two weeks later and has fully recovered. And no, it wasn't really that simple.

But I will never forget that fear, the sense of isolation, the terror of feeling as if I would be left behind and alone, if she died. Who would help me? And no, we have never really sat down and talked it through but I know she understands. Little did I know how important her positive attitude through all of this would matter to me in a very short time.

A Time of Conflict, Loss and Hope

My life took a major turn over the next four years and I'm not sure how much I actually had to do with it. In early 2013, my right knee replacement began to go south. I could hardly walk, and the pain was brutal. Frankly, a lot of that year is a blur. As I began my school semester in September (part time), surgery was scheduled and I had to take an extended medical leave. I was angry and frustrated. As much as I was battling to keep my grades up, a piece of me feared that if I step away now, I'll never get back.

And literally, as I was recuperating from knee surgery in the hospital, my mother's congestive heart failure was worsening. The day I came home, I had to call for an ambulance to take her to the hospital. She couldn't breathe. And again, thank God for my extended family. Annemarie and George put me in a wheel chair and took me to ICU to see my mom. Over the next several weeks, as my knee healed, I took my mom shopping, to her doctor's appointments, cooked the meals and sat with her at supper.

I spent a good chunk of my life being very angry and resentful toward my mother. As I began to heal and recover, I also began to gain perspective on my life and my relationships with my family. I knew in those weeks of caring for my mom that she had done the best she could with what she had to work with. She had no frame of reference, no text book to help her to be able to help me when I went to her as a little girl and shared that I had been molested. I know now that her "anger" was fear. And as I sat across the supper table in a home she had lived in for decades, I could see how frail she had become. And I knew that I loved her. And being free of that anger was so important to me.

On December 5th, 2013, I stood at a public podium for the first time and said, "*My name is Tracey Medeiros and I am a suicide attempt survivor.*" We were at Bridgewater (MA) State University for their *You Matter* candle light walk and panel presentation for suicide prevention. Annemarie was now serving as the director of the Bristol County Regional Coalition for Suicide Prevention and the university had asked her to bring in a panel. The three speakers were Craig Miller, an attempt survivor, Rosie Walisever, a loss survivor (yes, that loss survivor) and myself. I don't know how I got through it. And I don't remember much (but we do have it on film). But I do recall seeing the tears and the nodding heads in the audience when I shared my story. I knew from that moment that I could make a difference. I was overwhelmed with the hugs from students and faculty.

And yet, and this is so important for parents and loved ones of people with borderline personality disorder, PTSD, bipolar, etc. Within an hour of that moment, I was in a rage and I'm not even sure why. I vaguely recall that I had been struggling with fear and anxiety about my mom's health, being out of school, some issues at work, etc. and that with the insurance I had at the time, my medications were costing me a fortune, so I hadn't gotten refills...let's just say, the rest of the night is one to forget. But that can happen. It happens way less now because I am more alert and can catch things quicker (thank you, again, DBT).

As we stepped into 2014, my mom's health got worse and worse. We made countless trips to the hospital with the 911 calls. At the same time, Annemarie was working with Craig and Zak Swain to finish up a documentary that we were all involved with, *A Voice at the Table*. I really felt out of place with, like I didn't belong beside the others in the film. Craig had written a book. I saw Cara Anna's film clips. She is an international journalist. And then I saw Dese'Rae's work online (*Live Through This*)! I just didn't feel like I fit into this group.

Annemarie would constantly say during the filming and long after, that my voice was exactly what was needed – the everyday person, not someone with "rock star" status; that the majority of attempt survivors need to see and hear someone just like them. It was like that old saying I have heard, someone needs to be the quarterback, the leader; but the success depends upon the team's every day players. I was on the team.

I have still never met Cara, but I felt an immediate connection to Dese'Rae when we finally met. That is one awesome person! And Craig has always been considerate and kind. I know today that I "fit in" to the attempt survivor crowd, at least a bit.

And the 2014 story continues.

In February, I called the ambulance one last time. My mom was back in the ICU and the doctors made it clear there was nothing more they could do. So, I sat with her, held her hand and waited. She told me that I was the one kid (of six) she didn't have to worry about because she knew that *"Annemarie will take care of you."* I didn't know whether to laugh or cry. The first thought the crossed my mind was, *"She really does like Annemarie!"* I thought she hated her. You know, that parent thing: why can you help my kid get well and I couldn't? And I knew without any doubt that my mom loved me.

Through the tears, I repeated her words. *"Yes, Annemarie will take care of me."* She fell asleep. I left to get some supper…and she died. I went back home, curled up and cried.

The next few months are really lost to me. I just showed up. In March, I received a Leadership Award for my work in suicide prevention in Bristol County at a legislative breakfast. It was hard to accept. I wished my mom was there to see it. My oldest brother came. He always stepped in. In April, we screened *A Voice at the Table* (www.avoiceatthetable.org) at our state conference (2014 Massachusetts Conference for Suicide Prevention) and then shared it across the world on social media. The film was a call to action to welcome the voices of suicide attempt survivors to the education, prevention and intervention suicidology tables. It was very well received. Two weeks before that, the American Association for Suicidology (AAS), at its 2014 conference, announced it was forming a new division for suicide attempt survivors under the guidance of Dr. DeQuincy Lezine. (laughing out loud) I had no idea that we would be hanging out with him just a year later in Colorado.

In May of that year, we (Annemarie, Craig, Zak and I) co-hosted a public screening of the film at St. Thomas Church in Taunton. The pastor, Fr. Richard Bardusch, was, and still is, one of our biggest cheerleaders. It was a small gathering but included the director and assistant director of the MA DPH (department of public health) Suicide Prevention Program and some local leaders. The local paper, *The Taunton Daily Gazette*, did a full front page cover story about my story. That was weird to see. And I remember Annemarie telling me some time later that the National Suicide Prevention Lifeline was going to add the film to their new attempt survivor site: http://lifelineforattemptsurvivors.org/ and I said, "Really?" I was still having trouble grasping that people thought our little film was important. I don't have that problem anymore.

Later that summer, I took some time off to visit my step-kids in Indiana, dragging Annemarie along for company on the ride. I had rented this log house that turned out to be another "sanctuary," tucked in the middle of forests on one side and acres of corn fields on the other. The first morning there, we thought we'd take a walk in the woods and stopped dead in our tracks when we saw the "Be Alert for Bears" sign.

I was still grieving the loss of my mom and being with Jason and Jessica and their families was a great comfort. While we stay in touch via social media and the phone, I realized how much I missed them. Since that visit,

I've given a great deal of thought to either buying or building something in the Madison IN area to be able to visit more often. Annemarie did what she always does while I was spending time with the kids – she works, or writes, or reads, or works. It was a bit of a challenge because Internet access was a problem.

Every night, we'd listen to the coyotes wail and howl. We had a 13 hour drive home in front of us, so we decided to leave around 4:00 am. We had almost everything packed and were making the last trip out to the car, and the coyotes sounded very, very close. On the last trip from the house, Annemarie shut off the outdoor lights and walked down the porch to the car. She missed a step in the dark. In the middle of her yelling and swearing, we could hear the coyotes coming closer. I'm laughing and yelling at her to get in the car. She's crying and laughing and muttering something about spilling her Diet Coke. The coyotes are howling. Somehow, she dragged herself into the car, not sure if she hadn't broken an ankle or knee (with all the pain). And then we just sat there until she said, "*I need to pee,*" through her laughter. "*Too bad,*" was my response and peeled out of there into the darkness. The ankle was sprained and her knee has never been quite the same. The rest of 2014 was all of the "firsts." The first Thanksgiving without mom. The first Christmas without mom. There was also a lot of good that happened. And I was beginning to see that there was some emotional balance in my life, and that I can handle a crisis well. I still miss her a lot and wish she was here to enjoy this conversation.

That Pesky "C" Word

The title of this section is *Moving On.* 2015 felt more like I had smacked into the wall and stopped moving. Things began OK. Work was going well, I was still helping with the kids at the teen center. We were very busy with our community based suicide prevention and awareness work, hosting more community conversations and trainings. We were doing more local cable access shows. And, after spending a lot of time in 2014 developing the curriculum, we had finally begun to host our first series of wellness check workshops for suicide attempt survivors further along the healing path (Re-Energize & Re-Connect).

We presented that new program in April at our 2015 state suicide prevention conference and had been accepted to present the same panel at Colorado's Bridging the Divide Summit in May in Denver. It was on that road trip that Annemarie began to tape me for this conversation/book. And this might be a good time to share that working with a new therapist and counselor for a few years, having the correct mental health diagnosis and being on the right meds and right dose of those meds, was paying off. I was beginning to feel almost "normal," whatever normal is for me. Don't misunderstand, I still had times of feeling depressed and withdrawing from everyone and everything, but those times were very, very brief.

A couple of years before, I had a lumpectomy to remove what the surgeon called "tiny, embryotic cells" that had not yet formed into cancer. No big deal. Day surgery. But because of that, I received that annual please-come-in-and-let-us-crush-you-into-a-steel-plate card, and reluctantly did. Within a day, I got a call to come in for an ultrasound, which led to a surgeon and oncologist and a schedule for another lumpectomy. One side. One breast. Less than a week later, it was, would you please come back, we want to run more tests. Within another week, I was sitting in a room with Annemarie there for support and to take notes/ask the questions I might forget, to hear options. We came out with a surgical date the following week for a double mastectomy.

Being in shock can sometimes be a good thing and denial can work well once in a while.

I'm not going to go over every detail of the next 18 months. It was not fun. I tried very hard to not project with the "what ifs." It was textbook, stay in the day, stay in the moment, one day at a time. I had a great team at Dana Farber Boston (St. Elizabeth's Hospital), a radiation oncologist who was compassionate and direct, and a great team over at Dana Farber South Shore Hospital where I did the last of my treatments and follow up.

I went into surgery with my Minion "Stuart." And have a huge collection of Minions now. I got tired of being sick and having no energy. I was shocked when I lost my eyebrows (I expected the hair, but must have missed the eyebrows/eyelashes memo). I also missed the memo that when all of your lymph nodes under one arm are malignant and removed, the caution about what to do and not with that arm are forever; there's no, it will get better. I posted every move on Facebook and cannot tell you how grateful I am for everyone who cheered me on. It really does matter. There were some challenges. I was getting used to hearing, "Wow, we've never seen anything like that before." Really? I got really tired on not being able to breathe well or walk any distance.

A word to anyone else who has a double mastectomy. Watch out for those bumps in the road. Riding back and forth to the hospital every week was agony. The doctors said "it might be uncomfortable." Understatement. You should really tell women it hurts like hell and your eyes will water from the pain.

We found out I was that one in a million who is allergic to Tamoxifen. That was an unpleasant experience and hospitalization, to say the least. And no one believed that's what it was until Annemarie went home one night and sat and read those papers they include with medication. You know, the ones that are in about a 6 point font, and pages long as it unfolds? Well, way at the end, there was a description of "rare" reactions. Described me to a "T." "Wow, we've never seen anything like that before." Really?

But I do need to share my encounter with stigma. We were coming home form one of the every other week fluid procedures to keep me from dehydrating and I just started to slam the steering wheel. It might help to know that when I used to do that, Annemarie often wondered if we were going to go off the road. I was in tears, swearing, furious. Annemarie calmly suggested that we stop right now at a local restaurant and talk things out.

I took some breaths and said to her, "*People have been tripping over themselves to help me in any way they can since I shared that I had cancer and had to have a double mastectomy. Can I clean the house? Cook? Drive you anywhere? Where the F--- were they all when I wanted to kill myself?*"

She barely whispered to me, "*Welcome to the world of prejudice and discrimination. Welcome to stigma about attempting suicide.*"

I really thought I understood about that prejudice and discrimination. I mean, she always brings it up in trainings and public awareness events from her own experience. When she shares that she is a cancer survivor, people applaud. When she shares that she is visually impaired because of untreated skull fractures from domestic violence and hasn't been behind the wheel of a car for decades, people get quiet. When she says that her every day work is suicide prevention, people clear the room. I've heard her say that more times than I can count, but I never **felt it** like I did now. Wow! What an eye-opener.

Resilience. Interesting word and I heard it over and over during my cancer battle. For people who've known me most of my life that may not be the first word that comes to mind. You know that game we all play? What's the first word that comes into your mind when we say a person's name? I suspect most people might respond with angry, violent, unpredictable, but not resilient. And yet that's what I kept hearing from the entire cancer team. Resilient. Me? Really? I began to wonder if maybe I was somehow transforming from a "survivor" of many things to someone who can now take life as it comes and hold on to hope that it will get better.

The good news was that right after surgery, I moved in the "sanctuary" I talked about in the beginning of this conversation. My mother's will required that the family home be sold. There was a lot of work that had to be done and it took more than a year. In October 2015, as I began aggressive chemotherapy treatments, I moved into the McKinstry House, a 270-year old colonial that serves as the rectory for the Episcopal Church of St. Thomas. (laughing out loud) Yeah, me, living in a rectory. There's a spirit about this house that you have to feel. Words don't do it justice. And there was no better place for me to begin the long process of fighting the breast cancer diagnosis. Complete quiet in the middle of a city. A sanctuary, finally. The very first morning I woke up there I felt the difference. No yelling. No doors slamming. No tension. Wow!

To everyone's surprise, I returned to work part time as soon as I could. The agency was wonderful about allowing me time for my chemo and later, my radiation. It really helped to be back at work, even part time.

So, the obvious question hanging in the air like that 900 pound gorilla? Did I think about suicide? I was faced with a life threatening illness and even now, no one can promise me it's over. I had episodes of feeling depressed but they lifted pretty quickly because of the love and support around me and the coping skills I've learned to use every day, no matter what. I made a choice for life years ago. Suicide is not an option. Don't mistake that for the reality that I believe I will always have to deal with fleeting thoughts about suicide, but that does not mean I am suicidal any more. There is a difference and that's another piece of this life as an attempt survivor that I really don't think we talk about enough.

Annemarie was immersed in another documentary and I was able to help do some of the filming. I had to keep my distance from the teen center because of my compromised immune system, but they kept asking about me and sending hugs home. As 2016 began, we received word that one of our abstracts had been accepted by AAS for their 2016 conference in Chicago. I remember Annemarie sitting there staring at her laptop mumbling, "*It seemed like a great idea in October...*" (laughing out loud) Our panel was scheduled for April 1st. I'll just leave that there.

But for attempt survivors and their loved ones, I will share what happened in Chicago that was no April Fool's joke. I was excited and terrified. The crowd was huge and I never did feel as if I fully belonged there. By now, I had no hair, no eyebrows, no eyelashes. And I was struggling on the inside, trying to look "ok" on the outside. We were sitting in a panel presentation of attempt survivors with Dese'Rae and Amelia. I wrote a note and passed it over to Annemarie. It said:

For the last two weeks, I've been having suicidal ideations. Not sure where it's coming from and what's going on. I don't want to talk about at all. I have no plan. It's just feelings and thoughts. I'm telling you because it's the right things to do. And I have been taking my medication.

Yup! Right smack in the middle of a major conference, surrounding by people who could help me. I am a suicide attempt survivor who continues to heal, but no one ever said that "stuff" wouldn't still happen. And I'm not sure that we talk about those moments enough. The next afternoon, in spite of wanting to throw up with nerves, I sat on my own panel and presented about the importance of resilience to attempt survivors.

I wish everyone could hear Dr. John Draper saying, *"Suicidal thoughts do not a suicide make."*
I think it frightens families and loved ones of attempt survivors to think that we can get depressed, have some bad mood time, or even have thoughts of suicide, but that does not mean that we will act on that. I think of it as my "norm." It can be uncomfortable. But not always life threatening. That's why I still practice my coping skills. That's why I stay involved within the field of suicide prevention. That's why I love our monthly, spiritual wellness check workshop series. That all keeps me plugged into the positive.

The cancer battle has not ended. I developed an infection, was given steroids to combat it, but they wiped out what was left of my immune system. I developed a nasty blood infection and had to have surgery to remove a huge abscess from my stomach. That cost me another two months not working. And just when I thought it was safe, and I was getting ready to meet some friends for supper, I looked in the mirror and there was another abscess. The infection had returned. I fell apart. I just sunk down and cried.

Annemarie came in and found me sobbing. She covered it up with the medicated patches they had given me to use, gave me a hug, and gently nudged me out the door to have dinner with my friends, saying to me, "*Yes, you can…*" I had a wonderful night with my friends, the surgeon was able to take care of me in his office and I only lost a few days from work this time.

I am so done with cancer.

My hair has grown back – the eyebrows and eye lashes, too. And I am moving on.

There's one other point I need to make about cancer. I can't speak for guys who have been molested, but as a woman, we have those things called Pap smears. I have flat out refused to do one for longer than I can recall. It always brought back such bad memories of being molested. About 7 months into my healing from the mastectomy, I had my annual visit with my primary care doctor, and that "thing" came up. I never even blinked and said, yeah. Let's get it done. I hate cancer but I respect the damage it can do and I know I have to be very aggressive about my self-care. That includes the Pap smear. I'm sharing this for all the teens and young women out there who I know feel the way I did. Please, just do it. Get it done. Don't risk your life. That gives your abuser even more power of you. Don't let that happen.

And again, I hope you noticed there was no mention of suicide? It didn't happen. It never crossed my mind. Not fighting cancer was never an option. I made a choice for life a long time ago. I hope that sharing this helps someone else to make that choice, too. As Dese'Rae says, *please stay*. And I follow that up with you really do matter.

Random Wrap-Up Thoughts

So, we're in the midst of another documentary. This is the third film in the "voices" series, titled *Voices from the Shadows*. It's been interesting to follow the conversation in the film as it's been developing. The focus is the parents, family and friends of suicide attempt survivors, those who self-injure and those who still struggle with suicidal thinking but do not make an attempt.

We did some of the filming here at the house and one afternoon, Annemarie suggested that I sit down with the three moms. I could not imagine why the hell she wanted me to do that but, I did. And now I know why. The moms had questions about what they were doing and how they were doing it to help their loved ones that could only be answered by someone with this lived experience, a suicide attempt survivor. A 90-minute session turned into a three hour sit down.

I hope this doesn't come as a surprise, but the conversation ended up on DBT, again. One of the moms, Paula, shared that almost in desperation, she got Marsha Linehan's books and inhaled them. She discovered the same thing Annemarie did a few years ago. She was saying the wrong things, using the wrong terminology to try to communicate with her son. We kind of joked that all family members of attempt survivors might find DBT helpful, and I'll add that if you have a loved one who self-injures, please, please, get a hold of Dr. Barry Walsh's *Treating Self-Injury Second Edition*.

I came away from that session having a much better understanding of why we were making this film. The family members really need to have resources that cover so much more than how to recognize the invitations that someone may be suicidal. They need a lot more about long term self-care.

And a sort of companion project to this is one that I'm deeply committed to: bringing attempt survivors and loss survivors together. I've been talking about this ever since I heard Rosie share her story. We need to do more. I fully understand that in the very early days of grief from losing a loved one to suicide, loss survivors may not be ready to sit down and share stories with attempt survivors. Yet, every time I do share with a loss survivor or we have another community conversation and loss survivors are there, many have come up and said, "*I wish I had heard your story years ago.*" And I know they don't mean me, specifically. They mean attempt survivors.

That's why I was so glad when the loss survivors and attempt survivors from our wellness check workshops asked that we combine the groups into one. It's been helpful to hear the different points of view about some of the topics we discuss.

I hope this is a conversation that will continue.

And another conversation I hope will get more attention is self-injury. My experience has been that this is so misunderstood and suffers from the same negative attitudes of discrimination and prejudice (aka stigma) as suicide. The first time I sat in on a training by Barry Walsh, I was just stunned to hear someone talking about me and my story who really understood what I had experienced. I've lost track of how many of his presentations I've attended. If you are the parent, family, friend, whatever, of someone who self-injures, please – please go to one of his workshops, get his book, but get better informed.

I didn't cut as a kid, but I played the "Eraser Game," where we used an eraser on our arms until we bled, trying to erase ourselves away and see who could last the longest through the pain. I always won and that is not a good thing. I graduated from the Eraser Game to punching walls to hurt myself and to not hurt other people. I'd punch anything – the wall, a door, the car, school lockers were good targets. My pain was internal and manifested itself in an incredible rage. I had no idea why. I know now that I had buried the sexual assaults so deep, they didn't exist. But the anger and drive to hurt myself did. I know how hard it is for someone to understand, but the pain actually gave me some brief relief from the storm inside of me.

I didn't cut until I was a young adult. It got pretty intense. Afterwards, I would cry and cry so hard, I could barely breathe. I hated myself and everyone around me.

People who self-injure, kids or adults, need to know they are loved, they are not freaks. We need to do more to help this group and their families to not feel so isolated. That's why I never have a problem talking to our teen center kids or any other young people when they ask about my tats. Many adults on the other hand get a bit uncomfortable when they realize there are scars underneath the tats. Kids understand. They identify with my pain. My goal is to give them hope and encouragement to seek help.

The Home Stretch and
Wicked Awesome Wish List

In our spiritual wellness workshops (Re-Energize & Re-Connect), we often talk about the "Wicked Awesome Wish List." Everyone should have one. I've spent years dreaming about the three things I most wanted to do in my life.

In June 2016, June 3rd to be precise – my birthday, I finally bought the motorcycle that my brothers told me I would never have. You should have seen the look of horror on everyone's face around me. Seriously! Annemarie struggled her best to be "accepting" as she would say, but she really failed that one. But I will admit, when I got on it to ride it home, I was very, very nervous. And a few weeks later, I dumped it for the first time, but did it like I was taught and came out OK. People around me were really nice, checking to make sure I was OK.

Less than a month of riding and that blood infection I talked about grabbed me and I was out of work, mostly bed rest, and off the bike for two months. My first time back on the bike was in September 2016 for our annual "Light the Way" Suicide Prevention Motorcycle Run and Walk. I did OK. I rode with the Taunton Elks Lodge #150 Riders and they kept an eye on me. I'm looking forward to more time on the bike this summer.

One thing that really bothered me a lot was dropping out of college. And looking back I realize that it really was the best thing to do. I had another knee replacement, my mom got sicker and sicker and needed my help right up to the day she died. I was on another emotional roller coaster and would never have been able to do the work needed to pass my courses. I don't know if it's because of my mental health concerns or it's just me, I can't see that reality at the time it's happening, in the moment. I felt like a failure, again.

So, November 2016 was a pretty busy month for me. I returned to college to complete my degree in psychology with a focus on addictions. I decided to do it with online courses, one course per semester. That decision was actually made for me. I am among the millions who are strangled by college debt. When I took the medical leave a few years ago and didn't return within a certain time frame, wham! The loans smacked me up the side of the head. After a very ugly hissy fit, I settled down and did what I could, pay for one course at a time. And I didn't know that my employer will reimburse me, so I can apply that for the course I take. I love my job as a Certified Peer Specialist but I've watched one job or promotion pass me by because I don't have that four year degree. It sucks, but there's not much any of us can do. Oh, and did I mention that now that I can focus more and have a better understanding of how to study, that I'm getting A's and B's? Me. Who would have thought? My last course was anthropology and I loved it. Wait? Did I just say I loved school? That would shock anyone who crossed my path in high school (laughing out loud).

Once upon a time, I was a tiny young girl, right into my 20's. I stand five foot nothing and was a buff athlete. Between shattering my knees as a corrections officer and all the medication I've been given, my weight got way out of hand. There is no diet or program I haven't tried. Just before my cancer diagnosis, I was talking to my primary about a referral to a gastric bypass clinic. And then, boom! Cancer. But I didn't give up. I waited the year suggested and while still in the Herceptin treatments, began to process of achieving this last item on my "wicked awesome wish list."

I had to wait another 30 days after my last Herceptin infusion, my surgeon gave me the date. March 16th, 2017. This has been a lifetime. But, but…just in case you think this all went smoothly…remember, I seem to be that one half of one percent person. Yup. I went for my post-op one week visit and everything was fine. The next night, there we were again in an emergency department ruling out a blood clot. I was in excruciating pain, couldn't walk, and one of my legs was four times the normal size. I now introduce myself to doctors as "Hi. I'm the one half of one percent." With gratitude, I am delighted to share that I somehow, in bed sleeping, tore some muscles in my upper thigh. Right? What the hell? How do you do that? A little bed rest, heating pad and I was fine within a few days.

And that's a good thing, because we're about to hit the road to Phoenix, Arizona, and the 50th conference for the American Association of Suicidology. Can't miss that, right?

The Next Chapter

Since I've achieved my top three on the "wicked awesome wish list," what's next? Damned if I know.

I know I have a long journey ahead with the weight loss. The surgery is just the first step. Now it's about changing my whole way of thinking about food and healthy eating. I think I've heard that somewhere before, that behavior modification deal. Time to revisit DBT.

Achieving my psychology degree is important, And I know it doesn't change who I am as a person (or, at least, I hope not), but I need that "paper" to help open doors for things I do want to pursue in the field of suicidology.

So, I guess I need to give this more thought. And talk about at our next wellness check workshops. That's one thing on my new wish list, to bring or little workshop series to more attempt and loss survivors. And to do more to bring both of those groups together more often, and their family members, loved ones and friends. Ok, wait. I think I have some items on my new wicked awesome wish list.

I hope this conversation made some sense. If you're a teen or young adult, I hope it gave you hope to not give up. Stay. If you're an attempt survivor, remember that the label is not who you are. It's a part of your life that will continue to help you grow, but it does not define you.

And I do hope that you will step up and speak out. You are not alone.

I can't believe I finally got this all out. That was a lot of talking.

I matter. And you matter. And we need to let others who have attempted know that they matter, too.

One Last Thing

And this is how conversations with me go, really. "Oh, by the way…"

Coloring.

Maybe it's me but when I'm at a meeting, or training, or a workshop at a conference, no one seems to have a problem if someone in the room is knitting or crocheting, right? Why don't we give that same acceptance to people like me who honestly do focus better and do hear everything, but we need to color or doodle?

I color because it gives me a sense of direction and accomplishment. It also provides me with focus when I know I have a hard time focusing on a conversation, a TV show, or just wanting to read a story in a book. I started to color when I was younger and I really liked how it made the picture look as I was coloring it. That's where the feeling of accomplishment comes into play.

For a long time all I could find was kids' coloring books. I stumbled upon this website called stuff2color, and as I looked through it I found it had some challenging things I could color as an adult. It was introduced in DBT and I fell in love with coloring again. It's an important coping skill for me. I'm not ignoring you as you talk, present, or train, I'm actually much more attentive than if I have to sit there twiddling my thumbs and fidgeting because I just cannot sit still for long trainings, etc. Coloring helps ease my anxiety. It helps to calm me down.

After my mom died, Annemarie took me up to the White Mountains for Mother's Day and just let me sit there, looking out at the mountains and color. That's how I spent the entire weekend. It helped me to grieve in my own way. We (I) introduced coloring to our wellness check workshops and now everyone colors!

OK, I'm done now.

From my DBT classes:

Be patient toward all that is unsolved in your heart

And try to love the questions themselves

Like locked rooms and like books that are written

In a foreign tongue.

Do not seek answers which cannot be given to you

Because you would not be able to live them.

And the point is, to live everything.

Live the questions now.

Perhaps you will gradually,

Without noticing it,

Live along some distant day into the answer.

~ anonymous

References

Cameron, J. (2002). *The artist's way: A spiritual path to higher creativity.* New York: J.P. Tarcher/Putnam.

Lamott, A. (1994). *Bird by bird: Some instructions on writing and life.* New York: Pantheon Books.

Linehan, Marsha M. (2105) *DBT skills training manual second edition.* New York: The Guilford Press.

Walsh, Barent W. (2012). *Treating self-injury, second edition: a practical guide*. New York:The Guilford Press.

www.avoiceatthetable.org

www.traceymedeiros.net

If you or anyone you know is at risk and needs help, call:

1-800-273-8255 (TALK)

Push 1 for Veterans.

https://suicidepreventionlifeline.org/

Crisis Text Line:

Text "connect" to 741741

Resources:

http://www.suicidology.org/

http://livethroughthis.org/

Made in the USA
Middletown, DE
18 January 2019